Wind Rhymes

Poetry from the Breeze

By Carolyn R. Parsons

Photographs

by April Lindfors

ENNA Imprints

Written by Carolyn R. Parsons

Photography by April Lindfors

Cover photograph by April Lindfors

National Library of Canada Cataloguing in Publication Data

Carolyn R. Parsons

Wind Rhymes, Poetry from the Breeze

ISBN   978-0-9865006-0-2

0986500607

ENNA Imprints is a Canadian Publishing Company

This book is dedicated to the memory of my father

Harold Johnson Parsons

His life is my greatest inspiration

Introduction

It is with great pride I introduce you to my poetry. Wind Rhymes is a collection of poetry first written for publication on my blog, at www.breezedaze.blogspot.com. It is a collection of observations, thoughts, beliefs, judgements and simple writing practices.

You will find sonnets, minutes, sestinas, free verse and just plain prose on a variety of topics. It is a labour of love and the fulfilment of a life-long dream. I write in many different genres but poetry is my first love.

My influences for this poetry were found in nature, in life, from my family, my children, my darling husband, Kent, the love of my life and from the reminiscences of my home town, Change Islands, Newfoundland. Its boundless beauty inspires me daily even as I live far away.

The beauty of rural Ontario, where I now reside, inspires my current life and plays a great part in my writing as well. Rolling farmland and green lush fields wrap me in their warmth daily.

I hope you enjoy reading the words within this book as much as I enjoyed writing them.

Contents

LIFE

This section of the book is about life in general. It was inspired by observations made on a daily basis, about friends, family, relationships, spirituality, human nature, the sadness, the happiness and all of the places in between in the human psyche.

Life is a journey. It's about making mistakes and moving forward with the lessons learned. At this writing my 6 year old daughter Sophia is working on some math homework. She is a perfectionist and when she makes a mistake she gets upset with herself.

We all do this of course and my words to her, and to you are, life is about mistakes, we all make them, the goal is to learn from them, fix them where we can and then move on to the next thing. Mistakes aren't just incidental, they propel us forward in life and are essential for growth.

The following pages may even contain mistakes, as this is my first book of poetry, I'm unsure as to how to do it exactly. I am still very proud of it and I'll learn from the errors on these pages and improve in the next volume.

I hope you find some reflection of yourself and your life in this section.

Insomnia

Zombie-like the coffee drips and slurps
its aroma wafting from a favourite cup
two am, three am, four am, five
Admit defeat and finally give up

Exhausted yawns that yield no restful sleep
bone-tired body that refused to rest
noisy beeps, disturbing sounds of night
patience once again put to the test

No real reason, many many reasons
sleep avoids like an embarrassed friend
fatigue trips gaily down your eyes
and teases them with thoughts of daytime's end

Midnight desperate forages for comfort
nothing sooths the beast at the door
interrupting days and nights alike
leaving crumpled pages on the floor

Deprivation of the vital essence
we hopelessly pray our souls to keep
as we try again in vain at midnight
dreading never lay me down to sleep.

Dust to Dust

The dust that was the ancient knights
is scattered round and round
while the dust that was the Pharaohs
is washed along the ground

The dust that was the ancient prophet
blows betwixt the stones
while dust that was the peasant man
has blended with his bones

The dust that will be you and me
will blow with the gentle wind
and we'll be where we've never gone
and then come round again.

The dust that blows along the desert
once blew on the moor
for all is dust and all will be
as it has always been before.

The Divine Thread

There is a silver thread of life
weaving a patterned unity
I now can see that thread of light
the thread of divinity.

It's interwoven through ourselves
a silken tapestry
keeping us in a sacred bond
of love and unity

It runs amongst the living now
and those that once were here
translucent and invisible
and colourless and clear

Once I saw the thread in me
and knew I was divine
I felt that I was sacred
and that divinity was mine

But the day that made the thread appear
in its most precious hue
was the day that I first saw the same
divinity in you.

For we are one, we are the same
sharing this filament of silver
its light runs through all humanity
and bonds us all forever.

This subsection deals specifically with my struggle to make sense of life in a spiritual way. My beliefs are very personal and my entire life has been a journey towards compassion and inner peace.

There is no anger in these pages although some of the words may suggest that there might be. *After Broke Back Mountain*, for example, was written after I viewed that movie. It moved me and I was inspired to write my views and ponderings on the hate that was propagated by the characters in the film.

Achievements Downfall is a reflection of my internal battle between what our society suggests I should believe and what feels like truth to me.

Depression is not my journey but my observations of a close friend's battle with the disease.

Limbo is mine, I've been there, stuck, and fortunately I've moved forward but the memories of those days are fresh and the lessons learned from them are precious. There is a close relationship between Limbo and Depression.

This section is full of the light and dark and places in between and is a small representation of how life can be.

The Way

How deep they run, these soul saving echoes
vessels mined empty of independent gold thoughts
desperation voids quickly its waste-laden vessels
into an ocean of unfinished oughts

Dogma knocks loudly, testing the waters
with shake of the head and a smile of pure peace
knowledge of truth requires no fathers
the spirit encourages ego's release

The waters are still in the lakes of the prophet
simple the words, profound the great truth
the roof of the church bears tissue-paper soffits
just one breath of nature will flatten its roof

The virtues are posted on the door of a shrine
while the silent prophet whispers "this voice is mine".

Deceit of the Righteous.

With the word of the prophet in print
obedience demanded! Proceed! Jump!
His Latin melody shrouded in violet
bread and spirits measured by the litre
outside golden spires announced by the organ
through the brass pipes the liars music blows

The masses huddle inside as it blows
finding no escape though the print
of their feet walk with the tune of the organ
while every starving bone of their bodies jump,
begging, mister spare a litre
of water, hands, feet, meanwhile cold and violet

In unpardonable sin the liar in violet
pronounces fire and brimstone as the poor wind blows
pouring the blood from the golden litre.
The only one with the words in print
fearing the masses will learn the truth and jump
abandoning the purple and that melancholy organ!

The perfect melodic noise of the organ
hides the deceit and sin of the violet
The lies hidden where love-babes jump
and the ocean screams and the north wind blows,
nature and God angered at the print
of lies told to the people who drink from the litre

Angry mobs will smash the litre
into the priceless discords of the organ
and in fiery pyres burn the print
that support the falsehoods of the violet
and silent then the golden pipe blows
and the liar stripped naked, prepares to jump

The crowds in justified anger agree, Jump!
Now they swagger sober, free of the litre!
The wind of love and truth now blows
the melody of peace drown the sound of the organ
and the iris grows gently a soft violet
while a new harmony is found in the print.

On nature's demand an honest wind blows
and all must walk a firm path or jump.
The tabloid is the form of the print
as long as the patriarch offers the litre.
Change the course so the beauty of the organ
is never lost in the lies of the violet.

After Brokeback Mountain

Regular life shuns the curse
For what you are we give no permits
uneven wants and even worse
rainbows can't illuminate closets

Ridiculed in history's pages
accept the needs, deny the self
accepted by the gentle sages
yet seek psychological help

We'll cure you with these newfound methods
fix you up and mend your errors
you'll be normal, have a family
just avoid eye contact with mirrors

Baseball cards with manly men
none of them dared deny their hate
covering self with loathing outward
reared against their girlish fate

In volumes of the brilliant Wilde
the mystery lies in pages bounded
out impossible within
timeless whispers never sounded

Sin again preaches the man
hypocrite of an exclusive club
heaven bound he preaches hate
the paradox the only rub

Murderous rage inflames the simple
hate stirred up by latent lust
can't kill ourselves that would be sinful
let's kill the ones that we mistrust

Leave the mystery in the pages
Holy book yields chronic lies
Peace and love preached by the prophet
contradict the hypocrite's cries

So important is the message
damned to hell the twisted same
why was there not a word once whispered
by the prophet that shares its name

Achievement's Downfall

Eyes closed but I'm awake; lucidity
rarely exits subconscious meditation
silence bills the expert called divinity
the bounty for the cost of all creation

Images play in random arcs and bows
aimless gifts of earthly memories stored
matter grey releases all it knows
and silence fills the chasm that was bored

Eyes opened but I'm asleep; enlightenment
accords the seated swain a chance to glimpse
the absence of the darkest soul's unsettlement
abandoning the pranksters and the imps

Paradoxical disquietude is defunct
silence evades even the saffron monk

The River

To the river I went
in the heat of the day
to the river of life
to wash the heat away

To the river I went
in the dark of the night
to the river of life
in search of the light

To the river I went
in the cold of the winter
to the river of life
seeking warmth and shelter

To the river I went
in the bloom of the spring
to the river of life
as the song birds sing

To the river I went
in the warmth of the summer
to the river of life
to lay down and wonder

To the river I went
in the colours of the autumn
to the river of life
and stared down to the bottom

To the river I went
every day
and the river of life
carried me away.

To the river we go
it's where we should be
the river of life
will set us free

The Broken Bridge

The voices whisper to the light
into the abyss they will walk
unconcerned about the approaching distance
between the hills and over the bridge
nature desperately seeks to preserve her harmony
and the land still dances with the ocean

But at the edge of the ocean
where the flash of the sailor's light
whirls in manufactured harmony
together lovers and spirits walk
on different planes to the same bridge
unaware of the presence of the distance

It seems the void of distance
presents no challenge to the ocean
her depths merely the bridge
from darkness into ambient light
as the lovers and spirits walk
in ignorant peace and harmony

The violence of the clouds in harmony
with the mountains appearing in the distance
make the lovers quicken their walk
and the spirits escape blithely over the ocean
as the source of the artificial light
shines on another, impostor bridge

And in the ruins they bridge
the catacombs, disrupt the harmony
add the night and extinguish the light
creating an unnatural distance
from the land to the ocean
disabling the lovers and spirits who walk

When the lovers and spirits walk
silently across the span of a different bridge
beside the dried up ocean
stripped bare and stealing the harmony
leaving nature in the distance
whilst lover and spirit together lose sight of the light

For even the ocean will not live to walk
where there is no true light and a broken bridge
The harmony of man and nature victimized by
insurmountable distance

Limbo

Adrift, floating on a world of is
watching all the empty clouds
swaying with the nowhere breeze
the day is fraught with a void of words

Sitting here in vacant space
nothing moving, no true fear
no direction, no permission
compass needle points nowhere

The place between before and after
the moment of lackadaisy
somewhere in the centre of
being sane and being crazy

Normal is superfluous
all I have is mere existence
being where I'm supposed to be
with no energy to go the distance

Moment by wasted moment
the world attempts to spin me gentle
and If I could I'd plead my case
instead I stay where things are simple

The fault line lies between here and there
lazy tectonics will not shift
ever mired in living limbo
awaiting the continental drift

Depression

It pours without stopping
drenching the dirt
mud runs in rivulets
revealing the hurt

Try to be noble
pragmatic and stoic
but the rain keeps on falling
drowning this poet

And the question is why
and the answer evades
the bright light of day
by its closely drawn shades

And the damp hurts the bones
while the misery falls
on the heads of the innocent
who did nothing at all

And the girls weep with horror
and the rest curl with pain
and the sky sends its gift
of never ending rain.

The Din of Silence

In the numbing noise of normalcy
the speeded people walk
hurrying through the silent noise
of erroneous electric talk

Fast like trample-threatened bugs
to some false destination
more and more and more its beacon
misleads the impulse of creation

Loneliness cascades the masses
drowns their crowded purpose
no depth of love dare intrude
the life lived at the surface

Then unbidden silence comes
and loneliness descends
upon the desperate noise-crazed masses
battling quiet until the end

And in the raucous din of silence
the truth speaks without voice
the harbinger of quiet peace
offers another choice

Silence seeks the searching soul
and the wise drink tranquility
They do not blindly follow chaos
and choose their silent legacy.

Vintage Dawn

Crimson and gold breaks the dawn
rusted and worn on the earth
tired and wasted on humanity
she resentfully repeats the birth

The unloved and unwanted day
grumbled and whimpered and wasted
no love for the red-sky beginning
the wine of the dawn goes un-tasted

The people in ego land wander
wanting the things that destroy
more and more they collect things
each day the dawn heaves a sigh

Yet the crimson red sky greets us forever
hoping for a glimpse of a scene
Where people who care for the sunlight
Choose to see her reflection in green

The sun continues to send love
This the earth each day discovers
and the dawn with her scarlet red hope
continues to hope she recovers

Where am I?

Where am I this cold, dark day?
This endless day of night
Where do I find that which is me?
The inner sacred light.

Where do I look for what I seek?
Where do I need to go?
In deepest, darkest, cold despair
where is my sacred soul?

In deepest darkest silence
is the self that you do seek
in quiet, peaceful solitude
you'll hear the sacred speak.

The Ring

Grab the ring
hang on tight
go with peace
live large, live right

You know the way
trust the joy
learn to die
while you're alive

Live in joy
Take a chance
earth is full of heaven
find a reason to dance.

Solitude Lost

The swirling sphere that is the earth
spins beneath my feet
most days I am unaware
and I walk along in happy oblivion
but there are days when I feel as though
I'll be swept off the face of the earth
whirling into that spinning tornado
tossed like a discarded empty jar
off into the abyss of the universe
floating free and alone
nothing pulling and tugging
nothing holding me fast
and some nights, when the moon is full
and the stars shine bright
The earth shakes beneath my feet
and on those nights, for a moment
I wish gravity would just let me go
so that I can, Garbo style
just be alone.

The Voice

The voice says, hello
here I am listen to me
but I listen to another
and go a different way.
No this way, not that
the voice says
I know the way

But I go along ignoring it
I don't know this voice,
I don't know where it's come from
and trust for this voice hasn't come yet
so I go another way

and as I stumble along the path
tripping over bramble and rock,
bruising and bleeding
the voice says
that's ok, you'll be fine
and I argue, no
I've hurt myself

and I move along another path
much the same
listening to another.
One after the other
they tell me to go
this way and that
tearing me asunder

the voice gets stronger.
Every time I send it away
it comes back louder
it says, that isn't the way
listen to me
I know the way.

And one day I stop
I listen, what are you saying voice?
Tell me where to go
tell me which way
And the voice that is mine
tells me
Go your own way.

A Day!

I've been given a day
to do new things
to seize opportunity
a new day, uncharted waters
I've been given a day
of sunshine and magic
to learn new ways
to play with my daughters
I've been given a gift
of time,
moments and hours
to do with as I please
Carpe Diem, I'll listen to Horace
yes!
This day I will seize!

Knowing

The ocean knows that the sky is blue
The clouds know the sky never ends
The birds believe in the great beyond
And the fish know they swim with their friends

The sound of the water against the shore
whispers the words of the wise
The rustling song of the blowing winds
is aware of the rising tides

The leaves on the trees of the maple
know that the bees buzz in fields
The butterfly's beauty and grace
is known by the mountains and hills

and the knowledge of all that is true
lies in the infinite spirit of you.

Understanding

Your words come at me like a knife
they first wound me to my core
and then I let them go deciding
you can't hurt me any more

So you try with actions then
to intrude into my spirit
but you find it filled with love
there's no room for worthless hatred.

Then you cast another stone
and I smile and walk away
you don't like to be ignored
and you hate me, so you say

Then I turn and see your eyes
and I see the pain that's there
hidden down beneath the anger
crouching underneath the fear

and I send you love and light
and hope some day you'll start
to take the love and light I send
and replace the hatred in your heart

Ocean Tide

The dead reach out for the dying
We are dying when we are born to earth
The moment of our death is predetermined
in the moment of our worldly birth

and whether decades are the fortune
or a babe with just one breath
whether lives are stolen in the violence
or if we choose our time of death

Death will claim us as it must
ours is just to wonder why
we're born, we live beside the ocean
and then eventually we die.

The dead are an ocean tide,
reaching out for the dying
and those left living on the earth
waste our breath on futile crying

Don't spend time in senseless weeping
live your life with hope and pride
appreciate the life that's yours
until you join the ocean tide

Time

It swarms and passes and swirls around
now, then and what is to be
ever in a tandem race
that will have the victory
I move along at lightening speed
and keep picking up my pace
running against a speeding foe
in an endless losing race.

I slow down and it slows down
I am gaining it appears
but time slides down a sloping hill
and quietly disappears

LOVE

This section is inspired by the loves in my life, my sweetheart, Kent, my children, my extended family.

But it goes beyond that. *In Sunshine and in Sorrow* was written the day the Cougar Helicopter crashed off the coast of Newfoundland, with only one survivor out of the 18 on board. The feelings of helplessness and the subsequent compassion that welled up for those impacted inspired the words. Sometimes, when there is nothing to do to help those impacted by life's knocks, reaching out to others around you is of great importance.

A Poem of Hope was written to my Aunt Christine who was facing a health challenge to let her know we are all here, holding her up in our hands and our hearts, so that she doesn't have to hold herself up and can concentrate on her continued journey to wellness.

Love of those we do not know, compassion for those we know are in pain, empathy for those who need an understanding ear, all are explored in the poetry of this section of the book entitled **Love**

What is this Love?

What is this love?
From where did it come?
How did it know where to find me?
How did it know it should stay?
What is this love
that sooths and consoles me?
Does it realise how my heart
fears that this love will drift away?

What is this love that intrudes
on the thoughts that are secretly held?
Invading a soul that is damaged
by the times when it lived in a void.
What is this love that rescues
and holds me in hands warm and kind?
It lifts me to gently caress
a soul that was vacant inside.

What is this love that surrounds
and intrudes on a life half lived?
It connects our hearts with the thread
of its sweet aching gentle embrace
what is this love that fulfills?
Bringing me the peace that I seek
It stills me when storms hurt my heart
landing a contented smile on my face.

Empathy's Purpose

Observe this droplet on my finger tips
wiped from eyes of saddest blue
pain filled pools of saline water
reflective of a disappointed you

Dampened cheeks, I will my heart
to pull the pain you hold so deep
into the heart that grieves for you
and happily your tears I'll keep

I feel you tremble as I hold you
weeping low like willow branches
mourning for the loss of dreams and
the failure of your second chances

Gentle tears that cleansed and ceased
disperse in time, your sobs abate
I hold the pain transfused to mine
and arrest the birth of futile hate.

Enduring Love

Virgin love in all its splendour spreads
a golden light on every place
and lays a translucent hue of rosie dust
over the eyes of the lover's face

and he responds with heart and body
begging to kiss the maiden fresh
with heart in hand and hand on heart
they stroll the avenue of flesh

As time and temper take their toll
the blush has faded, yet the love has grown
maturity adds depth and strength
that newborn love has never known

The lustre fades, twas but all surface
nothing deep in the novel lust
a deeper love has penetrated
built on time and thought and trust

The greying hair and slowing gait
the fading timbre of their voices
hands held tight in life's embrace
support the rightfulness of their choices

I Wasn't Loved

I lost my way, I felt no joy
I cried alone in pain
I screamed until my voice was hoarse
It seemed I screamed in vain

I wandered lost, wayward and wild
following a lonely path
I chose the roads others laid
paved with hate and wrath

I angered for the love I craved
and felt I wasn't worthy
and took along some friends of mine
and showed them little mercy

I hated for I didn't know
why for me no love existed
and it left me angry, dark and cold
bare and weak and twisted

And all I wanted all along
was the love that others claim
to replace the hatred in my heart
and remove my cloak of shame

And they were there, they could have loved
the child that once was me
the strangers who looked past my shoulders
and pretended they didn't see

See the human in the being
give a second chance
don't walk by your fellow man
without a second glance

Extend the hand of kindness
whenever you see the need
a singular moment of compassion
might be your greatest deed.

The Battle

Torpidity, my lassitude's mourner
despairs and stares in disbelief
retreats to a distant cerebral corner
overcome with cranial grief

Depressive incomprehensible anguish
ego-driven false despair
hesitant to ever relinquish
the right to melancholy care

Lassitude returns the victor
in the battle quietly waged
lassitude, torpidity's heckler
motivation the compass gauge

Lassitude empowered to nourish
propagates the quintessence flourish

Infinity

On the day that you first sang to me
the sun enveloped my soul
in its brilliant yellow warmth
my heart was finally whole

You read my soul and said you'd stay
the earth shifted a little to the right
and I shifted a little in your arms
closer for the long sweet night

On the day that you first sang to me
The sky settled in to stay
So did we my destiny
that perfect sunny day

You read my soul and said you'd stay
as Blue Rodeo played in the night
5 Days in May, ours is one
today, preordained and right

On the day that you first sang to me
I heard a sweet love song
drifting with the whitest clouds
trying to sing along

You read my soul and said you'd stay
This marks infinity
and I sing to you and you to me
in perfect harmony.

Go Lightly

Go lightly my friend
on the path of your life
help up your neighbour
lessen *your* strife

hand out to the stranger
open heart to your friend
helping your brother
pays off in the end

The power of giving
the energy of love
is as strong as an eagle
and as light as a dove

In Sunshine and in Sorrow

On days when the sun seems farther away
and its heat isn't warm on your head
on days when sorrow reflects a great loss
when you want back what you've already had

When the sorrow comes and the days are bleak
and despair is your daily friend
and the light of the sun is so hard to see
blocked by the clouds that roll in

When the ocean roars loud on the rugged shore
and mimics the hurt in your soul
when it's hard to feel the heat from above
underneath life's harsh, barren cold.

Reach for the light that shines from within
turn to your sacred self
It's inside you'll find the sacred divine
a deep, holy infinite well.

Your heart will tell you that to brighten your day
keep the faith, keep the hope, keep the peace
you'll offer a hug, you'll hang on to hope
and then ask "What is it you need"?

In sunshine I ask you "How may I help"
and in sorrow I ask much the same.
A prayer and a hug, compassion and love
bring light on the darkest sad day.

Reach out take the hand of the people you love
hold them close and offer your warmth
in sunshine and sorrow; it's the love that you give
that lightens your burden the most.

A Poem of Hope

In all the large vast universe
in all the unabashed space
we float along in oblivion
with a frown upon our face

We spin alone in silence
we wonder how to cope
but in all the endless universe
lies a thread of infinite hope

We hang on to the thread
one next to the other
golden threads grow stronger
when woven fast together

And we'll take the woven rope
and toss it out to you
hold fast you know we've got you
we'll gently pull you through

Love and Defiance

Beyond the hills of the land
the music of the lovers dance
and play the song of love
for the heart of the man
matches the adoration of woman
caring for the needs of their child

Then dusk falls and calms the boy child
and *he* comes in from the land
his eyes meet those of the woman
and in domestic bliss hearts dance
hers in ancient rhythm for the man
his quiet in steadfast masculine love

and their moments of love
go unmonitored by the almond-eyed boy child
who claims the heritage of the man
and holds the rights of the land.
Tonight the river of life will dance
and celebrate in the womb of woman

and the warm body of the woman
still held in the embrace of love
grows heavy with the life dance
until the birth of the girl child
with no claim to the land
steals handily the heart of the man

and the knowledge of fairness in that man
in devotion and pledged fealty to that woman
like in equal dispensation the love
discharges this precious land
in equal dispensation betwixt child
in a new and modern dance

and the moon celebrates the dance
and large is the pride of the man
less is the conflict betwixt child
and greater the love of the woman
who has no knowledge of love
of that inanimate land

For the eyes of a child will dance
and land with respect on a man
who treats woman with equal love

NATURE

The Moon, the sun, the ocean, stars, trees, flowers, sunshine, rain, and fog, all of the elements of the outdoors feed my soul and are my muse. I live best in nature and believe that to be in tune with your surroundings is to be truly at peace.

Growing up next to the ocean was a blessing. Its greatness, the roar of its power as it bashed against granite shores still lulls me to sleep better than any lullaby could.

Within nature I find my deepest peace, my soul finds its greatest measure of strength from the outdoors, from the trees and the leaves and the sky. The moon pulls me forward and back and the sun warms my head and comforts my heart when it's broken.

There are no words, no combination of words I can create to describe the wonder this earth holds for me.

Sun Beams

Hot on my shoulder searing the skin
stroking the music that's playing within
fingertips dancing in rhythmic array
along my nerve endings at the cusp of the day

Sprinkled like salt on the edge of the street
frost patterned leaves dissolve from the heat
hot on my back burning like fire
leaving my senses full of desire

Hovering high like omniscient stalkers
watching the runners, the skaters, the walkers
heating my soul like a spark on the hearth
laughing and smirking with solarium mirth

These are the mornings of coffee and tea
mother earth shares her lover generously with me
and I lay here sated from the hot fingertips
sipping through love-bruised smiling lips

Dance with the Moon

She danced beneath the swollen moon
in anger and in pain
she stomped and screamed and railed and danced
and all of it in vain

She danced beneath the harvest moon
in sadness and in sorrow
she bent and bowed and bent again
and looked towards tomorrow

She danced beneath the crescent moon
in fear and worry twirled
with frightened eyes she thrashed about
and tried to flee her world

She danced beneath the bright new moon
in happiness and glee
she did a happy jig of joy
for all mankind to see

She danced the dance of ancient times
bending like a reed
and found she usually danced her best
when she let her partner lead

Fog

A drizzly weighty fog is all around me
heavy with its grey blue damp
aching deep within my bones
encompassing the wrought iron lamp

I stand in total darkness guided
by a beacon in the grey
guided towards a promised warmth
along the cobbles on the way

Stumbling forward into nothing
catching on the painful stone
upright, moving upward, forward
wandering lost but not alone

Gradually the fog is lifting
burned to air by rising sun
scars and wounds on hands are healing
as I start a happy run

Suddenly the light is on me
I stand in open fields of green
before me is the promised land
a place where peace and freedom reign

Where is this? I ask a stranger
is this heaven? Is this earth?
Yes it is, the stranger tells me
all are one and all are both

Find the light here on the earth
Go forth in peace and you'll arrive
Move with grace, compassion and mercy
learn to die while you're alive

The fog is only sent to lead you
without the fog you wouldn't go
Towards the light of peace and knowledge
or appreciate the glow

~Fog continued~

In darkest earthly days of fog
walk along with strength and purpose
Love and light and peace and knowledge
are always waiting near the surface

Ocean

How is it no camera's eye
can do justice to your briny blue?
no painter's brush can stroke the colours
that pay honest homage to your saline hue

Impotent words fall from the scribe
inadequate truth of the impression
No words of rapture, awe and wonder
no syllabus outlines such a lesson

Standing on your battered brink
I'm rescued from the silly notion
that we the egocentric mortal
can elucidate the transcendent ocean

Puppet Master

Hovering as a prop o'er a theatre stage
Romeo's pondering, what light is there?
hanging heavy in the heavens
invisible threads hold the sphere

Moving oceans with its strength
moving hearts to stand and stare
Its lustre steals the hidden light
of the sun's secret glare

The threat of moonlit madness lies
beneath the surface of the soul
lulled to lust and love and dance
excited by the lunar pull

Lovers hide in secret corners
mothers birth in hidden beds
witches dance to seek her favour
following the path the moon beam leads

Passions flare and senses heighten
when her greatness hovers near
children laugh and cry with fervour
there's nothing in the moon to fear

Hovering like a theatre prop
inconstant moon it envies nothing
master of the dancing puppets
as her solar lady sits in waiting

Weather Vane

Sallow winds blow at the clover
knocking over
grey earthen crocks
Weather vane cocks
spinning desperately around
ignore the ground
embrace the wind
Begin again
pick up the remnants of the storm
true to the form
We start anew
with cobalt blue
and bowing arches signify
storm has passed by
to still again
the weather vane.

Morning

Horizontal wind, impressive light show
Thunder booming, distant roar
early morning, before the sunrise
nature is knocking at my door

Cracking like a robin's egg
knocked from the nest a fragile parcel
the sky reveals its latest treasure
sailors delight is morning's marvel

Dawn breaks free from night's sweet chains
stretching yawning, a wrinkled newborn
robins peck in fresh-wash grasses
earth and day is ever reborn

Sunrise

Dark, grey, heavy
cold and dreary
weak and tired
bones are weary

Clouds come in
as they wont to do
and weigh their burden
heavy on you

Reach up higher
in search of light
attempt to win
without a fight

Drift to sleep
let go of things
dream of the hope
the sunrise brings

Lake Side Visit

Fields of aqua tinted waves
lap at shores of muted tan
sky kissed horizons smile gently
on the warmth of sparkling sand

Girl of blond plays darting dare me
with a tempting surf of bubbled edges
laughing with the older girl
with swirling, tangled brunette tresses

Sun gazed skin wet with droplets
footprints mar the smooth clay beach
sail boats drift across the distance
perfect dancers beyond our reach

Soaring seagulls voices muted
by the shouting lakeside's roar
swoop and take their place on buoys
snow white wings prepared to soar

Frosting clouds in a pretty pile
decorating blueberry skies
Divinity in every corner
inspires grateful quiet sighs

Row Boat

Enveloped within green heaven's leaves
floating adrift on the silent river
embraced by layers of coconut clouds
bluest sky that reaches forever
Above the water, an invisible current
convey the refrain of the people ashore
tacitly feathers float gently on water
released from the swans who swam here before

Peace descends and encompasses all
cloaking it in a love-skinned coat
as the river embraces and warms the island
and kisses the gunnels of the little row boat

Tea with the Queen

Loving queen of golden light
make me up some tea
I'm coming for a visit
will you sit and chat with me?

Tell me all the secrets
that I may be at peace
for my true nature is with you
and yours likewise with me.

The Golden Lady

The golden lady sits on high
and gently rules the land
she never scolds, she never wails
she never lays a hand

She sends her love to those below
ruling fast and fair
gracing one side then the next
to a simple rhythmic aire

She warms us all day after day
asking nothing in return
only those who take too much
will feel her gentle burn.

She waltzes gracefully on the clouds
in a dress of molten gold
and never takes a partner
for they're all too weak and cold

She is the golden lady
our solar queen above
she'll warm our lives and warm the earth
with everlasting love.

Magnolia

In the darkest grey dismal mist
that falls on the sodden grass
misery lingers in the silent home
enveloped in dingy splattered glass

Feverish and trapped in a wood cocoon
desperate for sunshine and air
claustrophobic and sighing in boredom
the raindrops don't even care

Then a glance through the tear stained panes
past the pond with ripples of rain
is the pale pink blossom of hope
sweet magnolia blooms once again

Short is the life they are given
yet long the imprinted impression
pale velvet discs of pure beauty
a brief life, too short for obsession

Whether long the life that is gifted
likewise a flower to blow in the wind
it's the wake of beauty we leave here
that matters utmost in the end

Mother Earth

She's lush and harsh and beautiful
amazing, large and awesome
Her generosity is endless,
her heart is pure and wholesome

She welcomes us to her gentle arms
is friendly with the skies
and cradles us in her gentle hands
as she sings us lullabies

She's our gentle blue-green mother
The rock of all our lives
though we don't appreciate
the very life she gives

Our mother is now weakened
sick with strange disease
and it's all because we've damaged her
with poison and with greed

Today is mother's day
a day marked in her honour
May every day be mother's day
let's harm our earth no further

Crystal Blue Persuasion

In infinite depths broke away
freed from the long-frozen source
floating adrift in saline fields
following a fate-charted course

The beauty is much on the surface
shades of white the visible hue
hidden beneath the strength of the tower
is crystalline infinite blue

Buoyed up by the laws of the mother
Layered in eons of mystery
captured by all and by none
pounded by earth's timeless history

In awe we are struck by the beauty
internally dwarfed by her depth
insignificance is our impression of us
as we stand in her magnificence

Such is the life that surrounds her
reflected in the blue Crystal mirrors
revealed in the profound glacial frost
is the truth that is ultimately ours

All the visible us is the finite
we're not just that part you can see
our lives mostly viewed at the surface
just observing the part that's called me.

Ignoring the truth internal
floating along in the sun
unaware of the aqua blue depths
at the essence of every one

Until the hot sun melts and diminishes
as the icebergs founder in the bay
and the heavy bottom unbalances
and the depth is revealed with a bang

Secrets cannot long stay hidden
The Crystal blue truth must be known
Snow covered, cold frosted egos
melt away and divinity is shown

Where is that Summer?

Where is that summer of love and of laughter?
salt water tears and happy ever after
It's drifted away on a tide and a prayer
sailing slowly away on wispy warm air

Free from the chains of the cold of the winters
Deep humid nights breathe of hot love and whispers
warm day slips gently into the dusk
waving its hand with a gesture of trust

The new day dawns bright a cooler-aired morn
and a crispness that belies its need to be born
slipping languidly into the colours of fall
scarlet canopies foreshadow slumber to all

The lustre of haze that fizzles and drifts
to dance with the sun at the edge of the cliff
then teeters and totters and falls with a crash
into the ocean with a soundless splash

This summer is gone with a silent sigh
leaving all of the people questioning why
nature blows breezes from out of the north
and encourages rest to the masses henceforth

The walkers tread heavily on crisp-crunched dirt
mulching the food that nourishes the earth
and they bundle up warmer and briskly walk by
as the earth whispers rest is the reason why.

And the summer slips sweetly into repose
on hammocks of cobwebs and snow flakey snows
but the promise of sunshine glosses its lips
and holds summers unlimited in its fingertips

MOTHERING

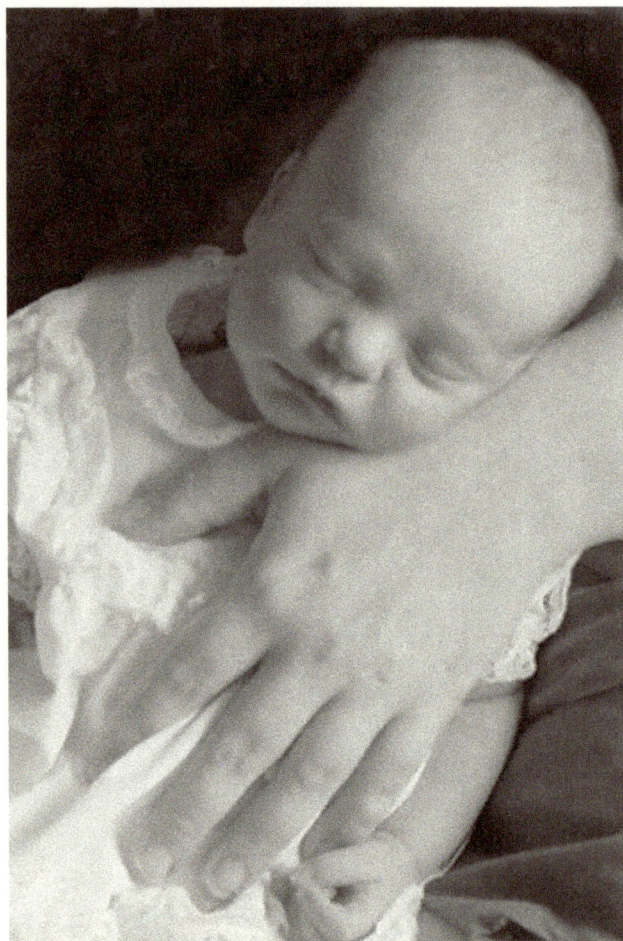

First and foremost I am a mother. My four daughters are my greatest teachers, from them I have learned the very important lesson of non-interference, defying the long standing idea that parenting is such hard work.

I've let go and decided to enjoy it in all its glory with no expectations other than my children become kind, compassionate and grounded individuals. So far so good!

The Journey to this point has been long and at times difficult and of course it continues. Along the way I have found that meditation, patience, chocolate chip cookies, red wine and a sense of humour have helped tremendously.

Balance

Leaning over the banister
poised to say good morning
she witnesses a miracle
a moment without warning

They flit around without her
independent in their movements
she watches wondering when they started
making such improvements

She backs away quietly
they really don't notice
ignoring mess and different ways
the mother changes focus

She slips into a different role
today she'll let them be
and let them make the mess they make
as they set their mother free

Perfection serves no purpose
the martyr ends up dead
loosen up the rigid rules
let them practice life instead

Mother free yourself from guilt
take time to live and be
you serve no one completely
unless you let yourself be free

Herself

She slipped into the silver gown
the one she wore each day
its silver threads and fabric
had begun to rend and fray

She checked the seams that held her in
and saw they'd ripped and torn
she knew the dress was useless now
the one she'd always worn

She slipped it off, discarded it
on the floor threadbare and worn
the remnants of her facade
ill-fitted, old and torn

There was no gown to mask her now
she stood in barest skin
and realised she felt herself
comfortable within

Authentic now she knew her skin
needed no silver gown
the Goddess that she knew she was
didn't even need a crown

This is the one I am she said
honest true and free
and she slipped into herself one day
and let herself just be

Dream Search

Outside the frosted pane looking back in
She sees her there, the girl that dreamt
of walking along the world's greatest wall
wiping the steam from wanting breaths
I peek at the girl with the visions
of standing in front of the Taj Mahal

She's writing her name in Sahara sands
and doing great things leaving all impressed
with the girl that did all she set out to do
nothing could stop the ambition she held
and then love crossed her path and detoured her dreams
as she paused and decided maybe a child or two

And she holds dreams in her head
while grasping her life in her hands
With baited breath waits for the life she proposed
and watches through tiny holes in the frost
made with her waiting breath and sees
all the dreams she dreamt are not as she supposed

Life in the moment bequeathed from the dreams
different and real and ever satisfying
the big life is little, opportunity passed
great walls and pyramids never realised
dreams pushed aside as the girl watches the frost
fill in the holes she made in the window pane's glass

While beside her the girls with the blonde happy curls
wipe holes in the glass and peer through the clearings
And see dreams in the trees and the ice covered branches
and the mother leans down and breathes their vision wider
smiling the children glance in wonder and dream
as the mother smiles down at her two second chances.

Eleven Minutes

In eleven minutes I'll wake you
and see your perfect faces
I'll marvel at your beauty
with sleep bedraggled traces

but now I sit with me
a gift so rare and fine
eleven minutes of solitude
as sweet as well-aged wine

In chaos I'll immerse myself
when it's your sweet morning
but first eleven minutes of solitude
at early morning's dawning

Quiet and peaceful beginnings
breath and meditation
eleven minutes of solitude
spent in sun salutations

Eleven minutes fading
it's time to awaken
I'm ready for your laughter
with just eleven minutes taken

The Gate

When it opened and you were free
it shook the very soul of me
Each sound you made outside the zone
left me screaming all alone

I used the gate to keep you in
and keep you safe and sound and then
you grew too big, you learned to scale
and you'd climb so fast it never failed

I removed the gate and watched you tumble
heart in mouth, ever so humble
as you picked yourself up and dusted off
and climbed again, to land so soft

Yet still each time I see you climb
my heart stands still, it stops in time
I've shown you how but you do it different
you scare me with your independence

I can't let go, I'm scared for you
but there isn't anything I can do
I'm helpless against the hands of time
it's hard to know you weren't ever mine

Love doesn't let me run away
yet it breaks my heart in two to stay
I hope some day you'll appreciate
how much it hurt to remove that gate.

The Girl

Emptiness is all around,
the shell of me is cold
I leap and dance and scream and wail
in a search to find my soul

And the whirling of the bitter winds
whips my heart to pieces
and blows me as a dervish
towards the precipices

The sun fights with the greying clouds
to spread her warmth on me
but the cold north wind says no, oh no
I will not let her be

Escape is not an option
there is no place to go
I'm trapped inside this barren cave
alone without my soul

and I weep for that broken girl
the one that didn't stay
I plead please send her back to me
Won't she please come back this way

I sit on the cold in Meditation
trying to drown out the din
the noise of electric cacophony
always seems to win.

Then the hand of love touches me
I'm here but where are you?
I know I am the bow of love
from my daughters' point of view

It's not so cold and empty now
myself creeps stealthily in
the sun breaks free from the clouds
its warmth touches my skin

And the sweetness of the child's voice
with the sunshine on my skin
unites with love and harmony
to make me whole again.

And the girl I thought was gone for good
came back with all the other
she hadn't gone at all she said
she had just become a mother.

Falling in Love

You've known her forever
yet suddenly you see
she's amazing and special
and incredibly unique

She's compassionate and loving
she's one of a kind
she's the love of your life
you never thought you would find

You've discover a way
of looking in her heart
and seeing the beauty
that sets her apart

Your surprise by the joy
falling in love brings to you
but you go with the feeling
it's exciting and new!

you get to know her better
as days go along
and you wonder how you missed it
how you didn't hear her song

Then you realise with wonder
she's the love, she's the one
she's the one you've been waiting for
now your searching is done

And you know you're complete
there is nothing else
when you finally fall in love
with your wonderful self!

Ma Donna Lisa

The Roman Terra holds the footprint of Giaconda,
She pulls gently the wagon full of love and contentment
Sharing her silks with the flotsam and jetsam
that surround the roadway to her appointment

Her voice in awe and bewilderment share with the child
the histories that lie in the countryside
where armies once battled when Rome ruled the world
though it is now the gentle habitat where artists reside

The bearing of nobility strains at her skin
while the heart in her chest beats renaissance
Contentment and peace are her constant companions
her fame and familiarity arrive only by chance

The oft studied face, the smile an enigma?
Perhaps just reflects the gentle heart of a mama.

Ode to Shiraz

The day has ended with a bang
and a few whimpers (from me)
The living room is destroyed
the carpet I cannot see
The dishwasher needs an emptying
To make room for a load
The floors need some cleaning
Very dirty is my abode
The kitty litter needs a scoop
Some mirrors need a shine
Some laundry needs some folding
But To hell with it, I need some wine

The Mirror

She traced them with her finger tips
fine lines of time and strife
tracked along her soft tanned face
that spoke of love and life

Memories etched in gentle canvas
set with the sheen of diversion
the face of intimate familiarity
reflects a life of full immersion

The mirror writes no fiction
it tells no soothing lies
it caresses those who care for truth
and accept the words it sighs

But a deeper authentic her is hid
her reflection holds an error
the self can only be seen by looking
into the spirit's magic mirror

MEMORIES

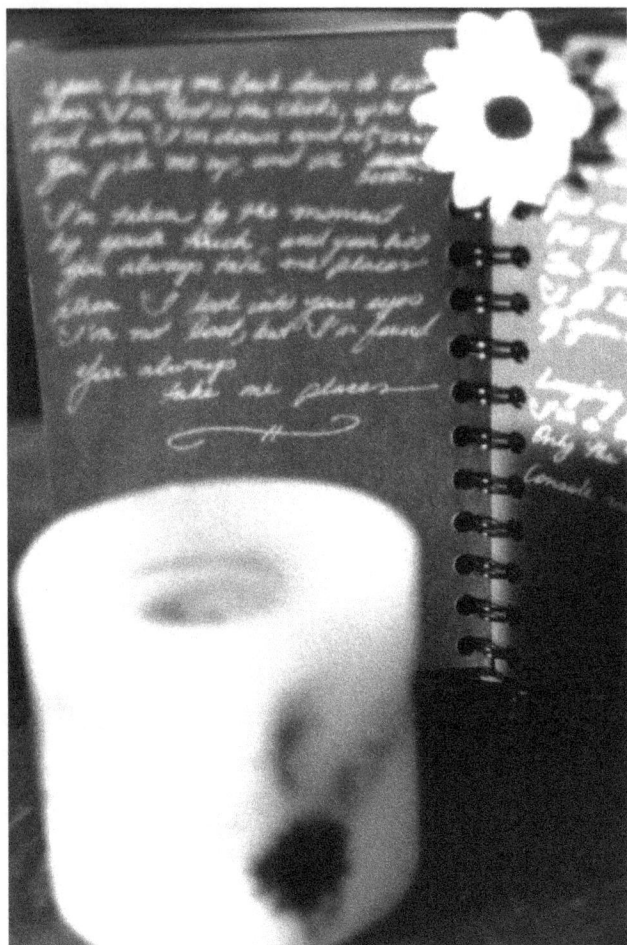

Childhood memories of my hometown, Change Islands, Newfoundland shaped my life and my soul. Life there was and still is simple and special.

The Atlantic surrounds this piece of rock in the ocean whose shores bear the answers to the mystery of the continental divide and whose people answer the mystery of life's true meaning. To live with nature, to take care of each other, to step up when need is great and to love and live and get along, the great mystery has a simple solution.

Charlie's poem, which was published in a Michael Jackson tribute anthology, is my refection on my teen years at Charlie and Mae's pool hall. We lost Charlie the same week Michael Jackson passed away, Mae had passed before. This poem is a tribute to them and those days.

Lady Blue was inspired by a childhood friend, Dona Hoffe, who introduced me to the music of Janis Joplin. I think of her whenever I hear any song by Janis and a recent conversation with her invoked this poem's birth.

The others are simply memories that bubble up at times begging to be recorded on paper. I listen to their urgings. I hope they inspire the reader to enjoy their own memories and perhaps these little poems will invite recall of old memories, for life is lived in moments and enjoyed in memories. That is all there is.

Childhood Memories

Bubbling up like champagne bubbles
sweet and tasty, vintage thoughts
drift outside of real life's troubles
free of all the shoulds and oughts

Simple times and pleasant places
ocean smells and soft, sponge turf
rocks with greying granite faces
white boats swaying at the wharf

Bluest blue of deepest brine
deadly tide delivers life
verdant nets of tangled twine
brings simultaneous ease and strife

Bubbling up like champagne bubbles
vintage thoughts, remembered deep
life of insignificant troubles
as I lay me down to sleep.

Charlie's Poem

Misty dew-dropped memories seep
like secret smiles on youthful cheeks
brightened by the dusk's red sky
shining on a youthful eye

Tripping down on gravelled pathways
towards the place where teen youths gather
dancing Thriller, zombie grooves
toeing moondance pop king moves

Shooting pool, in laughing halls
breaking up the marble balls
Pacman sings happy lament
to chocolate milk and cola drink

Quiet man behind the counter
smiling at a young boy's saunter
gentle woman gives advice
in a sweet familiar voice

Days gone by, teenage history
Quiet man now knows the mystery
gentle woman takes his hand
serenaded by the Thriller man.

Lady Blue
Bohemian heartbeat
genius of the damned
plucked from our lives
by Morpheus' hand

Blue lady Janis
in her Mercedes Benz
every sweet note
foreshadowed her end

Raw and uncensored
deep to the bone
lost in the crowds
while completely alone

Make my eyes weep
Cry baby cry
cat's gone to Africa
and I don't know why

Piece of my heart
somewhere man
held in the grip
of Lady Janis' hand

Demons chased you
until you caught them
drank of the poison
Capricorn stolen

Great lady Janis
singin' those blues
still busted flat
in Baton Rouge

Sings with white choirs
rocks with damned souls
Lady Blue Janis,
Ephemeral rose

Sandman

In the time of your alter universe
when you engage with the men of the sand
you cannot depend on his arms
to catch you before you land

If you think you are going to die
you will die before you awake
You'll land hard on the ground in a heap
and pray your soul he will take

If you think that you'll awake when you fall
it'll be exactly as you said
then instead of dead in a heap
you'll awaken and continue to dread

But if you know that you will take flight
when you fall in depths of the slumber
You will fly home to the light and the love
and live free in the land of the thunder

Imagination

In foggy lands the dragon flies
on clouds of dreams and cotton
while fairies dance in meadows green
in the land that time's forgotten

In misty lanes the lovers walk
in paths of dew and fragrance
while unicorns of white delight
canter in the distance

The fields of daisies hide the lairs
of creatures and of angels
while ghosts of trees and goddesses
are quietly entangled

So lies the land of fantasy
where witches sing with knights
that you will visit in your mind
when I turn out the lights

Serendipity

I travelled on a bumpy train, expecting dirt and mess
I found instead a feather bed, a place to lay and rest.

I walked into a rainstorm expecting to get wet
instead a yellow butterfly fluttered near my head

I kissed a handsome prince one day not expecting happy
after
I found to my intense delight happiness and laughter

I travelled on a gravel road, expecting many hills
Instead I found a gentle slope and pretty rolling fields

I thought life would be difficult but little did I know,
It isn't all that hard to live if you let it flow.

I walked along in worry, all the live-long day
and wasted time in pensiveness, when acceptance was the
way.

April Lindfors is a freelance portrait, event, and nature photographer. She has a special love for candid shots of everyday people, places, and events, and prefers shooting with traditional black and white film most of the time. April is also an aspiring singer/songwriter, poet, and blogger. She lives with her husband and two beautiful children in Largo, Florida. You can see April's work at www. a-muse-in-me.blogspot.com

Carolyn R. Parsons grew up on Change Islands, a little rural community on Newfoundland's North East Coast. She now resides in beautiful Tavistock, Ontario.

First and foremost she is a wife to her husband Kent Chaffey and mother to their four daughters Alyssa, Christina, Sophia and Martina.

She is a reporter for a local cable news magazine, First Local Stratford, moderator for Mothering Magazine's online community and an avid reader of both fiction and non-fiction.

As a writer, poetry is her first love but her first novel, Indigo is almost complete at this printing. It will be published in the fall of 2010.

www.ingramcontent.com/pod-product-compliance
Lightning Source LLC
Chambersburg PA
CBHW020950030426
42339CB00004B/29